M000222616

Spark

The One-Sentence Journal

xx Atticus

Andrews McMeel
PUBLISHING®

Also by Atticus

LVOE.
The Truth About Magic
The Dark Between Stars
Love Her Wild

Andrews McMeel Publishing
a division of Andrews McMeel Universal
1130 Walnut Street, Kansas City, Missouri 64106

www.andrewsmcmeel.com

23 24 25 26 27 SDB 10 9 8 7 6 5 4 3 2 1

ISBN: 978-1-5248-7742-2

Editor: Patty Rice
Art Director: Julie Barnes
Production Editor: Elizabeth A. Garcia
Production Manager: Tamara Haus

THESE SPARKS BELONG TO:

_____

✦

We all live
memorable lives—
sometimes you
just need
a little Spark
to remind you.

Letter from Atticus

Friends,

Before you get started, I wanted to introduce myself.
My name is Atticus, and this journal saved my life.

I am someone who has lived an adventurous life. And, as
such, I have always struggled with incredible highs and
devastating lows.

It was during one of these particularly low moments that
I decided to pull out a notebook and write down all the
happy thoughts I could think of. Every great memory,
accomplishment, and moment I could remember. Anything
that sent a Spark of positivity to my soul. After awhile,
I realized my sadness was gone. I had filled my mind with
so many positive thoughts that there was no more room
for sadness.

From then on, I found I kept coming back to that journal,
again and again . . . rereading each of my memories and
adding to them. Subconsciously creating a shield against
the sadness and ushering in inspiration to create more
memories, accomplish more goals, and strive for a bigger
and brighter life.

This journal was created to be that for you. A lifeline
filled with so much joy and hope that you will feel instantly
encouraged by just spotting it from across the room.
So don't stop once you've reached the last page; continue
to build your library of happiness in all the ways that
you've learned how.

That is my dream for you: that with each new memory you
add, your already beautiful life becomes a little brighter
and you never lose sight of the Sparks that light your soul.

Lots of love,

XX Atticus

MEMORY SPARKS

Use the prompt below to Spark a memory in one sentence.
Think about the who, what, when, where of each moment to
transport yourself back to that place and feeling.

YOUR SPARK: _May 2019_

EXAMPLE: _Sailing the South of France, drinking_
wine and laughing until our stomachs hurt.

FAN THE FLAME:

(Freewrite every emotion, feeling, thought, or joke
that this moment sparked in your memories.)

EXAMPLE: _I felt present and happy, like the day_
would last forever. The sun was perfect. The wine was
delicious. Megan's laugh was an envious soundtrack.
Traveling always reminds me of the joy life holds.

YOUR SPARK: _____

_____

_____

_____

FAN THE FLAME:

_____

_____

_____

_____

YOUR SPARK: _____

_____

_____

FAN THE FLAME:

_____

_____

_____

_____

_____

_____

YOUR SPARK: _____

_____

_____

FAN THE FLAME:

_____

_____

_____

_____

_____

_____

SPARK A FIREWORK

Choose one of your favorite and most powerful Sparks.
It can be an entirely new one or an old one from
previous pages. Now turn this Spark into a firework!

Write, draw, or doodle every detail that comes
to mind. Everything that made this memory special
and happy. Engage all of your senses. Step into
the memory like you're living it again, and pour
out everything you feel, see, and remember.
Fill it with joy!

MANIFESTING SPARKS

Let's explore the power of creative visualization.
Use the prompts below to visualize a future Spark
and manifest its light in your future.

FUTURE SPARK:

EXAMPLE: *I opened my wine business, and now I travel around the world tasting wines and importing them back home to our wine shop.*

FAN THE FLAME:

(How will accomplishing this make you feel?
Live within it like it's already happened.)

EXAMPLE: *Balanced, accomplished, successful, proud, inspired. I feel and know I can do anything. I'm traveling a lot, meeting new people. I feel busy, but my life is in control. This is life!*

"Give like the sun,
and the whole world
grows tall."

✦

4

FUTURE SPARK:

_____

_____

_____

FAN THE FLAME:

_____

_____

_____

_____

FUTURE SPARK:

_____

_____

_____

FAN THE FLAME:

_____

_____

_____

_____

SPARK A FEELING

Emotions are the most powerful tethers to past memories.
Using the prompts below, travel back in time
to when each of these emotions left its mark
on your memory and how it made you feel.

WHAT IS A MOMENT IN YOUR LIFE THAT SPARKED GRATITUDE?

_____

_____

_____

_____

_____

_____

WHAT IS A MOMENT THAT SPARKED EMPOWERMENT?

_____

_____

_____

_____

_____

_____

WHAT IS A MOMENT THAT SPARKED LOVE?

_____

_____

_____

_____

_____

_____

"Chase your stars, fool,

life is short."

"'Keep your head up,'
the old man said,
'for you are a lion.
Don't forget
that and neither
will the sheep.'"

SPARK YOUR SENSES

Your senses are one of the most powerful tools of
remembering. Have you ever smelled a scent, heard a song,
or tasted a flavor and it immediately brought you
back to a specific and special moment in time?
In this section, follow the prompts to ignite
your senses and Spark sensory memories.

SPARK SOUND:

(Write about a sound or song that reminds
you of a positive memory.)

EXAMPLE: *The Beatles always remind me of getting my
driver's license and driving around town with my friends.*

SPARK SMELL:

_____

_____

SPARK TASTE:

_____

_____

SPARK TOUCH:

_____

_____

SPARK SIGHT:

_____

_____

MEMORY SPARKS
Spark a memory in one sentence.

YOUR SPARK: _____

_____
_____

FAN THE FLAME:

_____
_____
_____
_____
_____

YOUR SPARK: _____

_____
_____

FAN THE FLAME:

_____
_____
_____
_____
_____
_____

YOUR SPARK: _____

_____

_____

FAN THE FLAME:

_____

_____

_____

_____

_____

_____

YOUR SPARK: _____

_____

_____

FAN THE FLAME:

_____

_____

_____

_____

_____

_____

SPARK A FIREWORK

Write, draw, or doodle your favorite Spark.

MANIFESTING SPARKS
Visualize future Sparks.

FUTURE SPARK:

_____

_____

_____

FAN THE FLAME:

_____

_____

_____

_____

FUTURE SPARK:

_____

_____

_____

FAN THE FLAME:

_____

_____

_____

_____

FUTURE SPARK:

_____

_____

_____

FAN THE FLAME:

_____

_____

_____

_____

"Set your life on fire.

Seek those who fan your flames."

—RUMI

SPARK A FEELING
Rekindle your emotions.

WHAT IS A MOMENT IN YOUR LIFE THAT SPARKED GRATITUDE?

_____

_____

_____

_____

_____

_____

WHAT IS A MOMENT THAT SPARKED EMPOWERMENT?

_____

_____

_____

_____

_____

_____

WHAT IS A MOMENT THAT SPARKED LOVE?

_____

_____

_____

_____

_____

_____

_____

"I'm tired of their stories,

let's write our own."

"I would rather have a body full of scars and a head full of memories than a life of regrets and perfect skin."

SPARK SOUND:

SPARK SMELL:

SPARK TASTE:

SPARK TOUCH:

SPARK SIGHT:

SPARK YOUR SENSES

Ignite your memories.

MEMORY SPARKS
Spark a memory in one sentence.

YOUR SPARK: _____

_____
_____

FAN THE FLAME:

_____
_____
_____
_____
_____
_____

YOUR SPARK: _____

_____
_____

FAN THE FLAME:

_____
_____
_____
_____
_____
_____

YOUR SPARK: _____

_____

_____

FAN THE FLAME:

_____

_____

_____

_____

_____

_____

YOUR SPARK: _____

_____

_____

FAN THE FLAME:

_____

_____

_____

_____

_____

_____

SPARK A FIREWORK
Write, draw, or doodle your favorite Spark.

MANIFESTING SPARKS
Visualize future Sparks.

FUTURE SPARK:

_____

_____

_____

FAN THE FLAME:

_____

_____

_____

_____

FUTURE SPARK:

_____

_____

_____

FAN THE FLAME:

_____

_____

_____

_____

FUTURE SPARK:

_____

_____

_____

FAN THE FLAME:

_____

_____

_____

_____

"I hope to arrive

at my death

late, in love,

and a little drunk."

✦

SPARK A FEELING
Rekindle your emotions.

WHAT IS A MOMENT IN YOUR LIFE THAT SPARKED GRATITUDE?

_____

_____

_____

_____

_____

_____

WHAT IS A MOMENT THAT SPARKED EMPOWERMENT?

_____

_____

_____

_____

_____

_____

WHAT IS A MOMENT THAT SPARKED LOVE?

_____

_____

_____

_____

_____

_____

"The right muse

will inspire truth

over imagination."

"She fell for
the idea of him

and ideas were

dangerous

things to love."

SPARK SOUND:

SPARK SMELL:

SPARK TASTE:

SPARK TOUCH:

SPARK SIGHT:

SPARK YOUR SENSES

Ignite your memories.

MEMORY SPARKS
Spark a memory in one sentence.

YOUR SPARK: _____

_____

_____

FAN THE FLAME:

_____

_____

_____

_____

_____

YOUR SPARK: _____

_____

_____

FAN THE FLAME:

_____

_____

_____

_____

_____

_____

YOUR SPARK: _____

_____

_____

FAN THE FLAME:

_____

_____

_____

_____

_____

_____

YOUR SPARK: _____

_____

_____

FAN THE FLAME:

_____

_____

_____

_____

_____

_____

✦

SPARK A FIREWORK

Write, draw, or doodle your favorite Spark.

MANIFESTING SPARKS
Visualize future Sparks.

FUTURE SPARK:

_____

_____

_____

FAN THE FLAME:

_____

_____

_____

_____

FUTURE SPARK:

_____

_____

_____

FAN THE FLAME:

_____

_____

_____

_____

FUTURE SPARK:

_____

_____

_____

FAN THE FLAME:

_____

_____

_____

_____

"Tell me the truth of you—the
mixed-up, muddled truth—and
I will tell you mine, and we
can be the secrets keepers
of each other's madness."

✦

SPARK A FEELING
Rekindle your emotions.

WHAT IS A MOMENT IN YOUR LIFE THAT SPARKED GRATITUDE?

_____

_____

_____

_____

_____

_____

WHAT IS A MOMENT THAT SPARKED EMPOWERMENT?

_____

_____

_____

_____

_____

_____

WHAT IS A MOMENT THAT SPARKED LOVE?

_____

_____

_____

_____

_____

_____

"Whatever seed you are, bloom."

"I have dreamed in my life, dreams that have stayed with me ever after; and changed my ideas; they have gone through and through me, like wine through water, and altered the color of my mind."

—EMILY BRONTË

SPARK SOUND:

_____

_____

_____

SPARK SMELL:

_____

_____

_____

SPARK TASTE:

_____

_____

_____

SPARK TOUCH:

_____

_____

_____

SPARK SIGHT:

_____

_____

_____

SPARK YOUR SENSES
Ignite your memories.

MEMORY SPARKS
Spark a memory in one sentence.

YOUR SPARK: _____

_____

_____

FAN THE FLAME:

_____

_____

_____

_____

_____

_____

YOUR SPARK: _____

_____

_____

FAN THE FLAME:

_____

_____

_____

_____

_____

_____

YOUR SPARK: _____

_____

_____

FAN THE FLAME:

_____

_____

_____

_____

_____

_____

YOUR SPARK: _____

_____

_____

FAN THE FLAME:

_____

_____

_____

_____

_____

_____

SPARK A FIREWORK
Write, draw, or doodle your favorite Spark.

MANIFESTING SPARKS
Visualize future Sparks.

FUTURE SPARK:

FAN THE FLAME:

FUTURE SPARK:

FAN THE FLAME:

FUTURE SPARK:

_____

_____

_____

FAN THE FLAME:

_____

_____

_____

_____

"Smile and let go.
It's just life after all
and you're doing it right
just by living."

SPARK A FEELING
Rekindle your emotions.

WHAT IS A MOMENT IN YOUR LIFE THAT SPARKED GRATITUDE?

_____
_____
_____
_____
_____
_____

WHAT IS A MOMENT THAT SPARKED EMPOWERMENT?

_____
_____
_____
_____
_____
_____

WHAT IS A MOMENT THAT SPARKED LOVE?

_____

_____

_____

_____

_____

_____

"Wine so delicately
pulls from us
all the stories
we hadn't planned
to tell."

"The beautiful thing
about young love
is the truth in our hearts
that it will last forever."

SPARK SOUND:

_____

_____

_____

SPARK SMELL:

_____

_____

_____

SPARK TASTE:

_____

_____

_____

SPARK TOUCH:

_____

_____

_____

SPARK SIGHT:

_____

_____

_____

SPARK YOUR SENSES
Ignite your memories.

MEMORY SPARKS
Spark a memory in one sentence.

YOUR SPARK: _____

_____

_____

FAN THE FLAME:

_____

_____

_____

_____

_____

_____

YOUR SPARK: _____

_____

_____

FAN THE FLAME:

_____

_____

_____

_____

_____

_____

YOUR SPARK: _____

_____

_____

FAN THE FLAME:

_____

_____

_____

_____

_____

_____

YOUR SPARK: _____

_____

_____

FAN THE FLAME:

_____

_____

_____

_____

_____

_____

SPARK A FIREWORK

Write, draw, or doodle your favorite Spark.

MANIFESTING SPARKS
Visualize future Sparks.

FUTURE SPARK:

_____

_____

_____

FAN THE FLAME:

_____

_____

_____

_____

FUTURE SPARK:

_____

_____

_____

FAN THE FLAME:

_____

_____

_____

_____

FUTURE SPARK:

_____

_____

_____

FAN THE FLAME:

_____

_____

_____

_____

"We are all just
the ghosts of stars
shining our little shine
back to the sky."

SPARK A FEELING
Rekindle your emotions.

WHAT IS A MOMENT IN YOUR LIFE THAT SPARKED GRATITUDE?

_____

_____

_____

_____

_____

_____

WHAT IS A MOMENT THAT SPARKED EMPOWERMENT?

_____

_____

_____

_____

_____

_____

WHAT IS A MOMENT THAT SPARKED LOVE?

_____

_____

_____

_____

_____

_____

"Beauty becomes
all the little things
that make our loves
exactly who they are."

"Sometimes, you have
to step outside of the
person you've been and
remember the person
you were meant to be.
The person you want to be.
The person you are."

—H. G. WELLS

SPARK SOUND:

SPARK SMELL:

SPARK TASTE:

SPARK TOUCH:

SPARK SIGHT:

SPARK YOUR SENSES

Ignite your memories.

MEMORY SPARKS
Spark a memory in one sentence.

YOUR SPARK: _____

FAN THE FLAME:

YOUR SPARK: _____

FAN THE FLAME:

YOUR SPARK: _____

_____

_____

FAN THE FLAME:

_____

_____

_____

_____

_____

_____

YOUR SPARK: _____

_____

_____

FAN THE FLAME:

_____

_____

_____

_____

_____

_____

SPARK A FIREWORK

Write, draw, or doodle your favorite Spark.

MANIFESTING SPARKS
Visualize future Sparks.

FUTURE SPARK:

FAN THE FLAME:

FUTURE SPARK:

FAN THE FLAME:

FUTURE SPARK:

_____

_____

_____

FAN THE FLAME:

_____

_____

_____

_____

"The truth about magic lies
in the very perfect fading wish
of every shooting star."

SPARK A FEELING
Rekindle your emotions.

WHAT IS A MOMENT IN YOUR LIFE THAT SPARKED GRATITUDE?

_____
_____
_____
_____
_____
_____

WHAT IS A MOMENT THAT SPARKED EMPOWERMENT?

_____
_____
_____
_____
_____
_____

WHAT IS A MOMENT THAT SPARKED LOVE?

"Powerful is the soul

that is beaten

but unbroken."

"You gave me an old book

that smelled of old glue

but more than that

it smelled of you

but not of you

the memory of you

because that's what smells

are supposed to do."

SPARK SOUND:

_____

_____

_____

SPARK SMELL:

_____

_____

_____

SPARK TASTE:

_____

_____

_____

SPARK TOUCH:

_____

_____

_____

SPARK SIGHT:

_____

_____

_____

SPARK YOUR SENSES

Ignite your memories.

MEMORY SPARKS
Spark a memory in one sentence.

YOUR SPARK: _____

_____
_____

FAN THE FLAME:

_____
_____
_____
_____
_____
_____

YOUR SPARK: _____

_____
_____

FAN THE FLAME:

_____
_____
_____
_____
_____
_____
_____

YOUR SPARK: _____

_____

_____

FAN THE FLAME:

_____

_____

_____

_____

_____

_____

YOUR SPARK: _____

_____

_____

FAN THE FLAME:

_____

_____

_____

_____

_____

_____

SPARK A FIREWORK

Write, draw, or doodle your favorite Spark.

MANIFESTING SPARKS
Visualize future Sparks.

FUTURE SPARK:

_____

_____

_____

FAN THE FLAME:

_____

_____

_____

_____

FUTURE SPARK:

_____

_____

_____

FAN THE FLAME:

_____

_____

_____

_____

FUTURE SPARK:

_____

_____

_____

FAN THE FLAME:

_____

_____

_____

_____

"Art has the answers
to many of the questions
we weren't brave enough to ask."

SPARK A FEELING
Rekindle your emotions.

WHAT IS A MOMENT IN YOUR LIFE THAT SPARKED GRATITUDE?

_____
_____
_____
_____
_____
_____

WHAT IS A MOMENT THAT SPARKED EMPOWERMENT?

_____
_____
_____
_____
_____
_____

WHAT IS A MOMENT THAT SPARKED LOVE?

_____

_____

_____

_____

_____

_____

"My love, it is a long way
from here to the stars, so let us
travel the rest as one."

"We all have our time machines, don't we. Those that take us back are memories . . . And those that carry us forward, are dreams."

—H. G. WELLS

SPARK SOUND:

_____

_____

_____

SPARK SMELL:

_____

_____

_____

SPARK TASTE:

_____

_____

_____

SPARK TOUCH:

_____

_____

_____

SPARK SIGHT:

_____

_____

_____

SPARK YOUR SENSES

Ignite your memories.

MEMORY SPARKS
Spark a memory in one sentence.

YOUR SPARK: _____

_____

_____

FAN THE FLAME:

_____

_____

_____

_____

_____

_____

YOUR SPARK: _____

_____

_____

FAN THE FLAME:

_____

_____

_____

_____

_____

_____

YOUR SPARK: _____

_____

_____

FAN THE FLAME:

_____

_____

_____

_____

_____

_____

YOUR SPARK: _____

_____

_____

FAN THE FLAME:

_____

_____

_____

_____

_____

_____

SPARK A FIREWORK

Write, draw, or doodle your favorite Spark.

MANIFESTING SPARKS

Visualize future Sparks.

FUTURE SPARK:

_____

_____

_____

FAN THE FLAME:

_____

_____

_____

_____

FUTURE SPARK:

_____

_____

_____

FAN THE FLAME:

_____

_____

_____

_____

FUTURE SPARK:

_____

_____

_____

FAN THE FLAME:

_____

_____

_____

_____

"Be twice as powerful
as you think you are."

SPARK A FEELING
Rekindle your emotions.

WHAT IS A MOMENT IN YOUR LIFE THAT SPARKED GRATITUDE?

_____

_____

_____

_____

_____

_____

WHAT IS A MOMENT THAT SPARKED EMPOWERMENT?

_____

_____

_____

_____

_____

_____

WHAT IS A MOMENT THAT SPARKED LOVE?

_____

_____

_____

_____

_____

_____

"Don't dream to live forever,

dream to forever live

while you're alive."

"If only we could
fall in love
with ourselves

as easily as we

fall in love

with everyone else."

SPARK YOUR SENSES

Ignite your memories.

SPARK SOUND:

_____

_____

_____

SPARK SMELL:

_____

_____

_____

SPARK TASTE:

_____

_____

_____

SPARK TOUCH:

_____

_____

_____

SPARK SIGHT:

_____

_____

_____

MEMORY SPARKS
Spark a memory in one sentence.

YOUR SPARK: _____

FAN THE FLAME:

YOUR SPARK: _____

FAN THE FLAME:

YOUR SPARK: _____

_____

_____

FAN THE FLAME:

_____

_____

_____

_____

_____

_____

YOUR SPARK: _____

_____

_____

FAN THE FLAME:

_____

_____

_____

_____

_____

_____

SPARK A FIREWORK

Write, draw, or doodle your favorite Spark.

MANIFESTING SPARKS
Visualize future Sparks.

FUTURE SPARK:

FAN THE FLAME:

FUTURE SPARK:

FAN THE FLAME:

FUTURE SPARK:

_____

_____

_____

FAN THE FLAME:

_____

_____

_____

_____

"Stop acting so small.
You are the universe
in ecstatic motion."

—RUMI

SPARK A FEELING
Rekindle your emotions.

WHAT IS A MOMENT IN YOUR LIFE THAT SPARKED GRATITUDE?

_____
_____
_____
_____
_____
_____

WHAT IS A MOMENT THAT SPARKED EMPOWERMENT?

_____
_____
_____
_____
_____
_____

WHAT IS A MOMENT THAT SPARKED LOVE?

_____

_____

_____

_____

_____

_____

"The hardest step
we all must take
is blindly trust
in who we are."

"What good are wings without the courage to fly?"

SPARK SOUND:

_____

_____

_____

SPARK SMELL:

_____

_____

_____

SPARK TASTE:

_____

_____

_____

SPARK TOUCH:

_____

_____

_____

SPARK SIGHT:

_____

_____

_____

SPARK YOUR SENSES
Ignite your memories.

MEMORY SPARKS
Spark a memory in one sentence.

YOUR SPARK: _____

FAN THE FLAME:

YOUR SPARK: _____

FAN THE FLAME:

YOUR SPARK: _____

_____

_____

FAN THE FLAME:

_____

_____

_____

_____

_____

_____

YOUR SPARK: _____

_____

_____

FAN THE FLAME:

_____

_____

_____

_____

_____

_____

SPARK A FIREWORK

Write, draw, or doodle your favorite Spark.

MANIFESTING SPARKS

Visualize future Sparks.

FUTURE SPARK:

FAN THE FLAME:

FUTURE SPARK:

FAN THE FLAME:

FUTURE SPARK:

_____

_____

_____

FAN THE FLAME:

_____

_____

_____

_____

"Love is here
and long away
in words and worlds unfolding."

SPARK A FEELING
Rekindle your emotions.

WHAT IS A MOMENT IN YOUR LIFE THAT SPARKED GRATITUDE?

_____

_____

_____

_____

_____

WHAT IS A MOMENT THAT SPARKED EMPOWERMENT?

_____

_____

_____

_____

_____

_____

WHAT IS A MOMENT THAT SPARKED LOVE?

_____

_____

_____

_____

_____

_____

"To love and be loved
is the true poetry of life."

"Alone we live

short rebellions

of death,

together

we defy it."

SPARK SOUND:

_____

_____

_____

SPARK SMELL:

_____

_____

_____

SPARK TASTE:

_____

_____

_____

SPARK TOUCH:

_____

_____

_____

SPARK SIGHT:

_____

_____

_____

SPARK YOUR SENSES
Ignite your memories.

MEMORY SPARKS
Spark a memory in one sentence.

YOUR SPARK: _____

_____

_____

FAN THE FLAME:

_____

_____

_____

_____

_____

_____

YOUR SPARK: _____

_____

_____

FAN THE FLAME:

_____

_____

_____

_____

_____

_____

YOUR SPARK: _____

_____

_____

FAN THE FLAME:

_____

_____

_____

_____

_____

_____

YOUR SPARK: _____

_____

_____

FAN THE FLAME:

_____

_____

_____

_____

_____

_____

SPARK A FIREWORK

Write, draw, or doodle your favorite Spark.

MANIFESTING SPARKS
Visualize future Sparks.

FUTURE SPARK:

_____

_____

_____

FAN THE FLAME:

_____

_____

_____

_____

FUTURE SPARK:

_____

_____

_____

FAN THE FLAME:

_____

_____

_____

_____

FUTURE SPARK:

_____

_____

_____

FAN THE FLAME:

_____

_____

_____

_____

"I found in you
what I found in me —
a great universe
I would spend a lifetime
uncovering."

SPARK A FEELING
Rekindle your emotions.

WHAT IS A MOMENT IN YOUR LIFE THAT SPARKED GRATITUDE?

_____
_____
_____
_____
_____
_____

WHAT IS A MOMENT THAT SPARKED EMPOWERMENT?

_____
_____
_____
_____
_____
_____

WHAT IS A MOMENT THAT SPARKED LOVE?

_____

_____

_____

_____

_____

_____

"In order to write about life,

first you must live it."

—ERNEST HEMINGWAY

"Love taught me
all I know

of happiness

and heartbreak.

Neither one

without the other."

SPARK SOUND:

SPARK SMELL:

SPARK TASTE:

SPARK TOUCH:

SPARK SIGHT:

SPARK YOUR SENSES

Ignite your memories.

MEMORY SPARKS
Spark a memory in one sentence.

YOUR SPARK: _____

_____
_____

FAN THE FLAME:

_____
_____
_____
_____
_____
_____

YOUR SPARK: _____

_____
_____

FAN THE FLAME:

_____
_____
_____
_____
_____
_____

YOUR SPARK: _____

_____

_____

FAN THE FLAME:

_____

_____

_____

_____

_____

_____

YOUR SPARK: _____

_____

_____

FAN THE FLAME:

_____

_____

_____

_____

_____

_____

SPARK A FIREWORK

Write, draw, or doodle your favorite Spark.

MANIFESTING SPARKS
Visualize future Sparks.

FUTURE SPARK:

_____

_____

_____

FAN THE FLAME:

_____

_____

_____

_____

FUTURE SPARK:

_____

_____

_____

FAN THE FLAME:

_____

_____

_____

_____

FUTURE SPARK:

_____

_____

_____

FAN THE FLAME:

_____

_____

_____

_____

"And for the first time
in a long time—
and maybe ever—
she was free."

SPARK A FEELING
Rekindle your emotions.

WHAT IS A MOMENT IN YOUR LIFE THAT SPARKED GRATITUDE?

_____

_____

_____

_____

_____

_____

WHAT IS A MOMENT THAT SPARKED EMPOWERMENT?

_____

_____

_____

_____

_____

_____

WHAT IS A MOMENT THAT SPARKED LOVE?

"Every word I write

is a breath

that keeps me alive."

"Too many die with
a brush in their hands,
a heart full of colors,
and a lifetime of
empty canvases."

SPARK SOUND:

_____

_____

_____

SPARK SMELL:

_____

_____

_____

SPARK TASTE:

_____

_____

_____

SPARK TOUCH:

_____

_____

_____

SPARK SIGHT:

_____

_____

_____

SPARK YOUR SENSES
Ignite your memories.

MEMORY SPARKS
Spark a memory in one sentence.

YOUR SPARK: _____

_____

_____

FAN THE FLAME:

_____

_____

_____

_____

_____

_____

YOUR SPARK: _____

_____

_____

FAN THE FLAME:

_____

_____

_____

_____

_____

_____

YOUR SPARK: _____

_____

_____

FAN THE FLAME:

_____

_____

_____

_____

_____

_____

YOUR SPARK: _____

_____

_____

FAN THE FLAME:

_____

_____

_____

_____

_____

_____

SPARK A FIREWORK

Write, draw, or doodle your favorite Spark.

MANIFESTING SPARKS
Visualize future Sparks.

FUTURE SPARK:

_____

_____

_____

FAN THE FLAME:

_____

_____

_____

_____

FUTURE SPARK:

_____

_____

_____

FAN THE FLAME:

_____

_____

_____

_____

FUTURE SPARK:

_____

_____

_____

FAN THE FLAME:

_____

_____

_____

_____

"Stay alive,

tomorrow is there

for those who wait."

SPARK A FEELING
Rekindle your emotions.

WHAT IS A MOMENT IN YOUR LIFE THAT SPARKED GRATITUDE?

_____
_____
_____
_____
_____
_____

WHAT IS A MOMENT THAT SPARKED EMPOWERMENT?

_____
_____
_____
_____
_____
_____

WHAT IS A MOMENT THAT SPARKED LOVE?

_____

_____

_____

_____

_____

_____

"Life is the art

of failing

magnificently."

"Vitality shows in not only the ability to persist, but the ability to start over."

—F. SCOTT FITZGERALD

SPARK SOUND:

_____

_____

_____

SPARK SMELL:

_____

_____

_____

SPARK TASTE:

_____

_____

_____

SPARK TOUCH:

_____

_____

_____

SPARK SIGHT:

_____

_____

_____

SPARK YOUR SENSES
Ignite your memories.

MEMORY SPARKS
Spark a memory in one sentence.

YOUR SPARK: _____

_____

_____

FAN THE FLAME:

_____

_____

_____

_____

_____

_____

YOUR SPARK: _____

_____

_____

FAN THE FLAME:

_____

_____

_____

_____

_____

_____

YOUR SPARK: _____

_____

_____

FAN THE FLAME:

_____

_____

_____

_____

_____

_____

YOUR SPARK: _____

_____

_____

FAN THE FLAME:

_____

_____

_____

_____

_____

_____

SPARK A FIREWORK

Write, draw, or doodle your favorite Spark.

MANIFESTING SPARKS
Visualize future Sparks.

FUTURE SPARK:

FAN THE FLAME:

FUTURE SPARK:

FAN THE FLAME:

FUTURE SPARK:

_____

_____

_____

FAN THE FLAME:

_____

_____

_____

_____

"We all have a little poetry to tell.
Stop your world and feel awhile."

SPARK A FEELING
Rekindle your emotions.

WHAT IS A MOMENT IN YOUR LIFE THAT SPARKED GRATITUDE?

_____
_____
_____
_____
_____
_____

WHAT IS A MOMENT THAT SPARKED EMPOWERMENT?

_____
_____
_____
_____
_____
_____

WHAT IS A MOMENT THAT SPARKED LOVE?

_____

_____

_____

_____

_____

_____

"I've spent a lifetime
stumbling around toward the
good person I know I can be."

"Listen to your heart before you listen to the world."

SPARK SOUND:

_____

_____

_____

SPARK SMELL:

_____

_____

_____

SPARK TASTE:

_____

_____

_____

SPARK TOUCH:

_____

_____

_____

SPARK SIGHT:

_____

_____

_____

SPARK YOUR SENSES
Ignite your memories.

MEMORY SPARKS
Spark a memory in one sentence.

YOUR SPARK: _____

_____
_____

FAN THE FLAME:

_____
_____
_____
_____
_____
_____

YOUR SPARK: _____

_____
_____

FAN THE FLAME:

_____
_____
_____
_____
_____
_____

YOUR SPARK: _____

_____

_____

FAN THE FLAME:

_____

_____

_____

_____

_____

_____

YOUR SPARK: _____

_____

_____

FAN THE FLAME:

_____

_____

_____

_____

_____

_____

SPARK A FIREWORK

Write, draw, or doodle your favorite Spark.

MANIFESTING SPARKS
Visualize future Sparks.

FUTURE SPARK:

_____

_____

_____

FAN THE FLAME:

_____

_____

_____

_____

FUTURE SPARK:

_____

_____

_____

FAN THE FLAME:

_____

_____

_____

_____

FUTURE SPARK:

_____

_____

_____

FAN THE FLAME:

_____

_____

_____

_____

"I don't know where I am going,

but I am on my way."

−VOLTAIRE

SPARK A FEELING
Rekindle your emotions.

WHAT IS A MOMENT IN YOUR LIFE THAT SPARKED GRATITUDE?

_____
_____
_____
_____
_____
_____

WHAT IS A MOMENT THAT SPARKED EMPOWERMENT?

_____
_____
_____
_____
_____
_____

WHAT IS A MOMENT THAT SPARKED LOVE?

_____

_____

_____

_____

_____

_____

"Her courage was her crown
and she wore it like a queen."

"Each beautiful thing we love
starts first
as the dirt
of dust and stars."

SPARK SOUND:

SPARK SMELL:

SPARK TASTE:

SPARK TOUCH:

SPARK SIGHT:

SPARK YOUR SENSES

Ignite your memories.

MEMORY SPARKS
Spark a memory in one sentence.

YOUR SPARK: _____

FAN THE FLAME:

YOUR SPARK: _____

FAN THE FLAME:

YOUR SPARK: _____

_____

_____

FAN THE FLAME:

_____

_____

_____

_____

_____

_____

YOUR SPARK: _____

_____

_____

FAN THE FLAME:

_____

_____

_____

_____

_____

_____

SPARK A FIREWORK

Write, draw, or doodle your favorite Spark.

MANIFESTING SPARKS

Visualize future Sparks.

FUTURE SPARK:

_____

_____

_____

FAN THE FLAME:

_____

_____

_____

FUTURE SPARK:

_____

_____

_____

FAN THE FLAME:

_____

_____

_____

FUTURE SPARK:

_____

_____

_____

FAN THE FLAME:

_____

_____

_____

_____

"My soul feels a hundred years old,

as if I've loved before

but can't quite remember."

✦

SPARK A FEELING
Rekindle your emotions.

WHAT IS A MOMENT IN YOUR LIFE THAT SPARKED GRATITUDE?

_____
_____
_____
_____
_____
_____

WHAT IS A MOMENT THAT SPARKED EMPOWERMENT?

_____
_____
_____
_____
_____
_____

WHAT IS A MOMENT THAT SPARKED LOVE?

_____

_____

_____

_____

_____

_____

"The first time I walked in Paris

there was a great remembering

of a thousand different dreams."

"'You could have been anything you wanted,' said the young boy to the old man in the mirror."

SPARK SOUND:

_____

_____

_____

SPARK SMELL:

_____

_____

_____

SPARK TASTE:

_____

_____

_____

SPARK TOUCH:

_____

_____

_____

SPARK SIGHT:

_____

_____

_____

SPARK YOUR SENSES

Ignite your memories.

MEMORY SPARKS
Spark a memory in one sentence.

YOUR SPARK: _____

FAN THE FLAME:

YOUR SPARK: _____

FAN THE FLAME:

YOUR SPARK: _____

_____

_____

FAN THE FLAME:

_____

_____

_____

_____

_____

_____

YOUR SPARK: _____

_____

_____

FAN THE FLAME:

_____

_____

_____

_____

_____

_____

SPARK A FIREWORK

Write, draw, or doodle your favorite Spark.

MANIFESTING SPARKS
Visualize future Sparks.

FUTURE SPARK:

_____

_____

_____

FAN THE FLAME:

_____

_____

_____

_____

FUTURE SPARK:

_____

_____

_____

FAN THE FLAME:

_____

_____

_____

_____

FUTURE SPARK:

_____

_____

_____

FAN THE FLAME:

_____

_____

_____

_____

"There is always a glimmer
in those who have been
through the dark."

SPARK A FEELING
Rekindle your emotions.

WHAT IS A MOMENT IN YOUR LIFE THAT SPARKED GRATITUDE?

_____
_____
_____
_____
_____
_____

WHAT IS A MOMENT THAT SPARKED EMPOWERMENT?

_____
_____
_____
_____
_____
_____

WHAT IS A MOMENT THAT SPARKED LOVE?

_____

_____

_____

_____

_____

_____

"Think only of the past as its
remembrance gives you pleasure."

—JANE AUSTEN

"Stay young,
stay brave,
stay wild."

SPARK SOUND:

_____

_____

_____

SPARK SMELL:

_____

_____

_____

SPARK TASTE:

_____

_____

_____

SPARK TOUCH:

_____

_____

_____

SPARK SIGHT:

_____

_____

_____

SPARK YOUR SENSES
Ignite your memories.

MEMORY SPARKS
Spark a memory in one sentence.

YOUR SPARK: _____

FAN THE FLAME:

YOUR SPARK: _____

FAN THE FLAME:

YOUR SPARK: _____

_____

_____

FAN THE FLAME:

_____

_____

_____

_____

_____

_____

YOUR SPARK: _____

_____

_____

FAN THE FLAME:

_____

_____

_____

_____

_____

_____

SPARK A FIREWORK

Write, draw, or doodle your favorite Spark.

MANIFESTING SPARKS
Visualize future Sparks.

FUTURE SPARK:

_____

_____

_____

FAN THE FLAME:

_____

_____

_____

_____

FUTURE SPARK:

_____

_____

_____

FAN THE FLAME:

_____

_____

_____

_____

FUTURE SPARK:

_____

_____

_____

FAN THE FLAME:

_____

_____

_____

_____

"To be a poet is
to set off to understand
and never arrive."

SPARK A FEELING
Rekindle your emotions.

WHAT IS A MOMENT IN YOUR LIFE THAT SPARKED GRATITUDE?

_____

_____

_____

_____

_____

_____

WHAT IS A MOMENT THAT SPARKED EMPOWERMENT?

_____

_____

_____

_____

_____

_____

WHAT IS A MOMENT THAT SPARKED LOVE?

_____

_____

_____

_____

_____

_____

"'Come on, darling,' she said.
'Let's drink wine and paint
our universe.'"

"She left him —
and began
on that day
a long-overdue
adventure within."

SPARK SOUND:

SPARK SMELL:

SPARK TASTE:

SPARK TOUCH:

SPARK SIGHT:

SPARK YOUR SENSES
Ignite your memories.

MEMORY SPARKS
Spark a memory in one sentence.

YOUR SPARK: _____

FAN THE FLAME:

YOUR SPARK: _____

FAN THE FLAME:

YOUR SPARK: _____

_____

_____

FAN THE FLAME:

_____

_____

_____

_____

_____

_____

YOUR SPARK: _____

_____

_____

FAN THE FLAME:

_____

_____

_____

_____

_____

_____

SPARK A FIREWORK
Write, draw, or doodle your favorite Spark.

MANIFESTING SPARKS

Visualize future Sparks.

FUTURE SPARK:

_____

_____

_____

FAN THE FLAME:

_____

_____

_____

_____

FUTURE SPARK:

_____

_____

_____

FAN THE FLAME:

_____

_____

_____

_____

FUTURE SPARK:

_____

_____

_____

FAN THE FLAME:

_____

_____

_____

_____

"In a poet's love
she would live forever,
if even for a moment
in that fading ink."

SPARK A FEELING
Rekindle your emotions.

WHAT IS A MOMENT IN YOUR LIFE THAT SPARKED GRATITUDE?

_____

_____

_____

_____

_____

_____

WHAT IS A MOMENT THAT SPARKED EMPOWERMENT?

_____

_____

_____

_____

_____

_____

WHAT IS A MOMENT THAT SPARKED LOVE?

_____

_____

_____

_____

_____

_____

_____

"Sometimes the best cure
for today is tomorrow."

✦

"As life goes on it becomes tiring to keep up the character you invented for yourself, and so you relapse into individuality and become more like yourself every day."

—AGATHA CHRISTIE

SPARK SOUND:

SPARK SMELL:

SPARK TASTE:

SPARK TOUCH:

SPARK SIGHT:

SPARK YOUR SENSES
Ignite your memories.

MEMORY SPARKS
Spark a memory in one sentence.

YOUR SPARK: _____

FAN THE FLAME:

YOUR SPARK: _____

FAN THE FLAME:

YOUR SPARK: _____

_____

_____

FAN THE FLAME:

_____

_____

_____

_____

_____

_____

YOUR SPARK: _____

_____

_____

FAN THE FLAME:

_____

_____

_____

_____

_____

_____

SPARK A FIREWORK

Write, draw, or doodle your favorite Spark.

MANIFESTING SPARKS
Visualize future Sparks.

FUTURE SPARK:

_____

_____

_____

FAN THE FLAME:

_____

_____

_____

_____

FUTURE SPARK:

_____

_____

_____

FAN THE FLAME:

_____

_____

_____

_____

FUTURE SPARK:

_____

_____

_____

FAN THE FLAME:

_____

_____

_____

_____

"And that is where I'd like to stay,
forever lost in Paris, left amongst
the lingered laughs of friends."

SPARK A FEELING
Rekindle your emotions.

WHAT IS A MOMENT IN YOUR LIFE THAT SPARKED GRATITUDE?

_____
_____
_____
_____
_____
_____

WHAT IS A MOMENT THAT SPARKED EMPOWERMENT?

_____
_____
_____
_____
_____
_____

WHAT IS A MOMENT THAT SPARKED LOVE?

_____

_____

_____

_____

_____

_____

"In the right love
we will discover new love
for ourselves."

"She was of
witches and wolves,
a wild and magical thing
impossible to hold
and harder to explain,
and I was forever and
always under her spell."

SPARK SOUND:

_____

_____

_____

SPARK SMELL:

_____

_____

_____

SPARK TASTE:

_____

_____

_____

SPARK TOUCH:

_____

_____

_____

SPARK SIGHT:

_____

_____

_____

SPARK YOUR SENSES

Ignite your memories.

MEMORY SPARKS
Spark a memory in one sentence.

YOUR SPARK: _____

_____

_____

FAN THE FLAME:

_____

_____

_____

_____

_____

_____

YOUR SPARK: _____

_____

_____

FAN THE FLAME:

_____

_____

_____

_____

_____

_____

YOUR SPARK: _____

_____

_____

FAN THE FLAME:

_____

_____

_____

_____

_____

_____

YOUR SPARK: _____

_____

_____

FAN THE FLAME:

_____

_____

_____

_____

_____

_____

SPARK A FIREWORK

Write, draw, or doodle your favorite Spark.

MANIFESTING SPARKS
Visualize future Sparks.

FUTURE SPARK:

_____

_____

_____

FAN THE FLAME:

_____

_____

_____

_____

FUTURE SPARK:

_____

_____

_____

FAN THE FLAME:

_____

_____

_____

_____

FUTURE SPARK:

_____

_____

_____

FAN THE FLAME:

_____

_____

_____

_____

"Embark today
on the grand adventure
that coud be
the rest of your life."

SPARK A FEELING
Rekindle your emotions.

WHAT IS A MOMENT IN YOUR LIFE THAT SPARKED GRATITUDE?

_____

_____

_____

_____

_____

_____

WHAT IS A MOMENT THAT SPARKED EMPOWERMENT?

_____

_____

_____

_____

_____

_____

WHAT IS A MOMENT THAT SPARKED LOVE?

_____

_____

_____

_____

_____

_____

"The road was

whispering to me again."

"The world only exists
in our eyes. . .
You can make it
as big or as small
as you want."

—F. SCOTT FITZGERALD

SPARK SOUND:

SPARK SMELL:

SPARK TASTE:

SPARK TOUCH:

SPARK SIGHT:

SPARK YOUR SENSES

Ignite your memories.

MEMORY SPARKS
Spark a memory in one sentence.

YOUR SPARK: _____

FAN THE FLAME:

YOUR SPARK: _____

FAN THE FLAME:

YOUR SPARK: _____

_____

_____

FAN THE FLAME:

_____

_____

_____

_____

_____

_____

YOUR SPARK: _____

_____

_____

FAN THE FLAME:

_____

_____

_____

_____

_____

_____

SPARK A FIREWORK

Write, draw, or doodle your favorite Spark.

MANIFESTING SPARKS
Visualize future Sparks.

FUTURE SPARK:

_____

_____

_____

FAN THE FLAME:

_____

_____

_____

_____

FUTURE SPARK:

_____

_____

_____

FAN THE FLAME:

_____

_____

_____

_____

FUTURE SPARK:

_____

_____

_____

FAN THE FLAME:

_____

_____

_____

_____

"They were bonded like two
stars, and neither would ever be
the first to let go."

✦

SPARK A FEELING
Rekindle your emotions.

WHAT IS A MOMENT IN YOUR LIFE THAT SPARKED GRATITUDE?

_____
_____
_____
_____
_____
_____

WHAT IS A MOMENT THAT SPARKED EMPOWERMENT?

_____
_____
_____
_____
_____
_____

WHAT IS A MOMENT THAT SPARKED LOVE?

_____

_____

_____

_____

_____

_____

"I'll meet you there

in that field

past the walls

of all these worries."

"Poetry
at the wrong time
is madness. Poetry
at the right time is
magic."

SPARK SOUND:

_____

_____

_____

SPARK SMELL:

_____

_____

_____

SPARK TASTE:

_____

_____

_____

SPARK TOUCH:

_____

_____

_____

SPARK SIGHT:

_____

_____

_____

SPARK YOUR SENSES
Ignite your memories.

MEMORY SPARKS
Spark a memory in one sentence.

YOUR SPARK: _____

_____

_____

FAN THE FLAME:

_____

_____

_____

_____

_____

_____

YOUR SPARK: _____

_____

_____

FAN THE FLAME:

_____

_____

_____

_____

_____

_____

YOUR SPARK: _____

_____

_____

FAN THE FLAME:

_____

_____

_____

_____

_____

_____

YOUR SPARK: _____

_____

_____

FAN THE FLAME:

_____

_____

_____

_____

_____

_____

_____

SPARK A FIREWORK

Write, draw, or doodle your favorite Spark.

MANIFESTING SPARKS
Visualize future Sparks.

FUTURE SPARK:

_____

_____

_____

FAN THE FLAME:

_____

_____

_____

_____

FUTURE SPARK:

_____

_____

_____

FAN THE FLAME:

_____

_____

_____

_____

FUTURE SPARK:

_____

_____

_____

FAN THE FLAME:

_____

_____

_____

_____

"All you have to do is write
one true sentence. Write the truest
sentence that you know."

−ERNEST HEMINGWAY

✦

SPARK A FEELING
Rekindle your emotions.

WHAT IS A MOMENT IN YOUR LIFE THAT SPARKED GRATITUDE?

_____

_____

_____

_____

_____

_____

WHAT IS A MOMENT THAT SPARKED EMPOWERMENT?

_____

_____

_____

_____

_____

_____

WHAT IS A MOMENT THAT SPARKED LOVE?

_____

_____

_____

_____

_____

_____

"Tomorrow brings hope
and coffee."

"In her heart and soul she set fire
to all things that held her back—
and from the ashes
she stepped into
who she always was."

SPARK SOUND:

_____

_____

_____

SPARK SMELL:

_____

_____

_____

SPARK TASTE:

_____

_____

_____

SPARK TOUCH:

_____

_____

_____

SPARK SIGHT:

_____

_____

_____

SPARK YOUR SENSES
Ignite your memories.

MEMORY SPARKS
Spark a memory in one sentence.

YOUR SPARK: _____

_____

_____

FAN THE FLAME:

_____

_____

_____

_____

_____

YOUR SPARK: _____

_____

_____

FAN THE FLAME:

_____

_____

_____

_____

_____

_____

YOUR SPARK: _____

_____

_____

FAN THE FLAME:

_____

_____

_____

_____

_____

_____

YOUR SPARK: _____

_____

_____

FAN THE FLAME:

_____

_____

_____

_____

_____

_____

SPARK A FIREWORK

Write, draw, or doodle your favorite Spark.